Karin Baron

HAMBURG

die Schöne the Beautiful

Ellert & Richter Verlag

Der Himmel auf Erden – in bester Citylage

Der Himmel auf Erden liegt in Hamburg mitten in der Stadt. Alster heißt er, denn dieses zum See gestaute Nebenflüsschen der Elbe ist es, das auf 182 Hektar den Himmel in die Stadt spiegelt und ihren Bewohnern zu Füßen legt. Ein paar Segelschiffe draufgetupft sowie die 120 Alsterschwäne, und fertig ist ein verkehrsberuhigtes lichtes Großstadtidyll, das unter Europas Metropolen seinesgleichen sucht.

Die Außenalster – das Ufer umstanden von hohen Trauerweiden, die Grünflächen ein einziger Landschaftspark, das Wasser gesprenkelt mit einer Armada von Booten und alle paar Hundert Meter ein Café mit eigener Steganlage. Das Beste daran: Bis auf einige private Villengrundstücke am nördlichen Ende ist das innerstädtische Biotop für alle zugänglich. Für Flaneure und ihre Hunde, für gestresste Businessmenschen, für Radfahrer – und für Hamburgs Jogger. Dass dicht am Wasser die beliebteste Rennstrecke für Freizeitsportler verläuft, behagt allerdings nicht jedem, der einfach nur spazieren möchte.

Eine imposante städtische Silhouette eröffnet der Blick von der Krugkoppelbrücke gen Süden, Richtung Binnenalster. Die Türme mehrerer Hamburger

Heaven on earth – in a prime city-centre location

In Hamburg, heaven on earth is in the heart of the city. Its name is the Alster, a lake formed by damming a tributary of the River Elbe. Covering an expanse of 182 hectares, its waters reflect the heavens into the city and place them at her inhabitants' feet. Add a few yachts dotted about and the 120 Alster swans and you have a traffic-calmed, bright, metropolitan idyll that is unparalleled among Europe's major cities.

The Aussenalster, or Outer Alster, has banks lined with tall weeping willows, green open spaces that merge into one big landscaped park, water sprinkled with an Armada of boats, and every few hundred metres a café with its own private landing stage. Best of all, apart from the gardens of a few grand private houses at the northern end, this city-centre biotope is open to all – to strollers and their dogs, to stressed business people, to cyclists, and to Hamburg's joggers. Admittedly, people who simply want to go for a walk are not always comfortable with the fact that the amateur athletes' favourite racetrack runs close to the water.

The view south from Krugkoppel Bridge toward the Binnenalster (Inner Alster) reveals an imposing urban silhouette. The towers of Hamburg's main churches

Ob Regatta oder Freizeitschippern, die Außenalster ist ein Paradies für Segler. Den Panoramablick über die innerstädtischen Ufer gibt's nicht nur vom Wasser aus, sondern auch vom Turm der St.-Michaelis-Kirche, dem berühmtesten „göttlichen" Wahrzeichen der Stadt.

Whether racing or yachting for leisure, the Aussenalster (Outer Alster) is a sailor's paradise. The panoramic view of the inner-city lake's shoreline can be appreciated not only from the water but also from the tower of St. Michael's, Hamburg's best-known "divine" landmark.

Die Außenalster, so charmant wie vielseitig. Von links oben im Uhrzeigersinn: die prächtigen Villen des gehobenen Bürgertums, die Steganlage des Cafés *Bobby Reich*, ein Mastenwald am Abend, nachdem auch der letzte Skipper von Bord gegangen ist, der baumbestandene Uferweg.

The Aussenalster is both charming and varied. Clockwise from top left: high-society mansions, the jetty of the *Bobby Reich* café, an eventide forest of masts after the last skipper has disembarked, the tree-lined lakeside path.

Idyll am Wasser und beliebter Ort fürs Dolce Vita auf Hamburgisch: der romantische Rundtempel im Eppendorfer Hayns Park am oberen Alsterlauf. Im 19. Jahrhundert gehörte er zum Besitz des Senators und Zweiten Bürgermeisters Max Theodor Hayn (1809–1888).

A waterside idyll and popular spot for the Hamburg-style dolce vita: the romantic round temple in Hayns Park, Eppendorf, on the upper reaches of the Alster river. In the nineteenth century it was part of the estate of Senator and Deputy Mayor Max Theodor Hayn (1809–1888).

In Stein gemeißelte Gediegenheit an der Binnenalster, Hamburgs „guter Stube“ – vom Alsterpavillon (ganz rechts), dem weltbekannten Café am Jungfernstieg, bis zu den imposanten Büro- und Geschäftsgebäuden am Ballindamm (links).

Die Türme von links nach rechts: St. Petri, St. Katharinen, St. Nikolai, der Rathausturm, die Alte Post und St. Michaelis, liebevoll „Michel“ genannt.

Substance and quality carved in stone around Hamburg’s “front parlour,” the Binnenalster (Inner Alster): from the Alsterpavillon (far right), the world-famous café on Jungfernstieg, to the imposing office and commercial buildings on Ballindamm (left).

The towers from left to right: St. Peter’s, St. Catharine’s, St. Nicholas’, the Rathaus (City Hall) tower, the Alte Post (Old Post Office) and St. Michael’s, affectionately known as the “Michel.”

Der Jungfernstieg, bekannteste Uferpromenade Hamburgs an der Binnenalster. Rund um den Alsterpavillon mäandern Caféhaustische und -stühle übers Pflaster, und von hier startet auch die weiße Flotte der Alsterdampfer.

The Jungfernstieg, Hamburg's best-known lakeside promenade, by the Binnenalster. Coffeehouse tables and chairs meander across the pavement all around the Alsterpavillon. This is also the departure point for the "white fleet" of Alster boats.

Hauptkirchen erheben sich über großkalibrige Geschäftshäuser und Hotels mit grün oxidiertem Kupferdach. Mittendrin der Turm des Rathauses im Stil der Neorenaissance und – 2016 fertiggestellt – der Konzertpalast und Stolz der Stadt, die Elbphilharmonie. Weithin sichtbar schlägt die kristallen funkelnde Hülle von Hamburgs neuem Wahrzeichen Wellen.
Eine Reverenz ans Wasser natürlich, denn das Wasser ist es, das Hamburg seine unverwechselbare Ausstrahlung verleiht und es zu dem gemacht hat, was es ist. Das Wasser und der Sinn seiner Bewohner fürs Geschäft. Ein bisschen was vom Hamburger Nass kommt von oben. Na, und? Was macht das schon, wenn einem der wunderbare graubraunblaugrüne Rest einfach so zu Füßen liegt. Das Hamburger Wetter ist jedenfalls weit besser als sein Ruf.
Der Hamburger selbst auch. Unaufgeregt ist er und diskret. Liberal, weltoffen und tolerant. Wer ihn für distanziert hält oder gar kühl, hat was falsch verstanden. Humor? Doch, hat er. Typ angelsächsisch, also eher trocken. Geld? Hat er auch. Muss er aber nicht zeigen. Was nicht heißt, dass er es zwingend für sich behält. Hamburg hat nicht nur die höchste Millionärs- und

rise above large-scale office buildings and hotels with green roofs of oxidized copper. Amidst them stand the tower of the neo-Renaissance Rathaus (City Hall) and the city's pride and joy, the palatial Elbphilharmonie concert hall, completed in 2016. With its highly visible location and sparkling glass shell, Hamburg's new landmark creates a stir.
Naturally, its design pays homage to water, because water lends Hamburg its unmistakable aura and has made the city what it is today, or rather water and Hamburgers' business acumen. Some of Hamburg's wetness comes from above. So what? What does it matter when you have the rest of this wonderful grey-brown-blue-green element at your feet? In any case, Hamburg's weather is better than its reputation.
As are Hamburg people. They are coolheaded and discreet, liberal, cosmopolitan and tolerant. Anyone who finds them distant or even cold has misunderstood something. A sense of humour? Yes they have, of the Anglo-Saxon type, in other words rather dry. Money? They have that too, but they don't feel the need to show it. Which does not mean that they necessarily keep it to themselves. Hamburg not only has the highest density

Hamburg-City: Das prachtvolle Hamburger Rathaus (rechts) mit dem grünen Kupferdach wurde 1886–1897 im Stil der Neorenaissance errichtet. Der belebte Gänsemarkt (oben) mit seinen Rotklinkerfassaden und dem Lessing-Denkmal bietet Shopping und Schlemmen gleichermaßen. Links der Neue Wall, edelste der Hamburger Einkaufsadressen.

The City: Hamburg's magnificent neo-Renaissance Rathaus (right) with its green, oxidized copper roof was built in 1886–1897. Bustling Gänsemarkt (top left) with its red clinker brick facades and monument to Gotthold Ephraim Lessing offers both shopping and eating facilities. Bottom left is Neuer Wall, the most upmarket of Hamburg's shopping areas.

Die strahlend weißen Alsterarkaden, hinter denen sich Hamburger Traditionsgeschäfte und -restaurants verbergen, bieten geradezu italienisches Flair. Nur die Schwanenflotte auf der Kleinen Alster beim Rathausmarkt verweist auf nördlichere Gefilde.

Shops and restaurants steeped in Hamburg traditions hide behind the gleaming white Alster arcades which have an almost Italian air. Only the fleet of swans on the Kleine Alster (Little Alster) next to the Rathausmarkt are a sign of more northerly realms.

Am Bleichenfleet mit seinen schwimmenden Restaurant-Pontons liegt die Alte Post. Für den 1847 vollendeten Bau aus unverputzten Ziegeln und Sandstein standen italienische Renaissance-Palazzi Modell.

Heute beherbergt die Alte Post eine Ladenpassage, die 1971 den Umbau der Innenstadt zu einem Passagenviertel einleitete.

Beside the Bleichenfleet canal with its floating restaurants stands the Alte Post (Old Post Office), completed in 1847. This bare brick and sandstone building was modelled on Italian Renaissance palazzi.

It now houses a shopping mall that in 1971 marked the start of the city centre's conversion into a district of covered shopping malls.

Nobel überdacht shoppen in Hamburger Passagen. Von links oben im Uhrzeigersinn: die *Mellin-Passage,* älteste der Stadt mit einer der schönsten Buchhandlungen Europas, das edle *Levantehaus* in der Mönckebergstraße, sowie in den Großen Bleichen die *Kaisergalerie* und das schwarz-weiß gestreifte Licht-Wunder *Galleria.*

You can shop in style in all of Hamburg's covered shopping malls. Clockwise from top left: the *Mellin-Passage,* the city's oldest mall with one of Europe's most beautiful bookshops, the upscale *Levantehaus* in Mönckebergstrasse, in Grosse Bleichen the *Kaisergalerie* and the amazing light effects in the black-and-white striped *Galleria.*

Cabriodichte Deutschlands. Hamburg gilt auch als die Stadt der Stifter und Mäzene. Alle zusammen pflegen sie ein lässiges Understatement. Nicht umsonst sind Gummistiefel die High Heels des Nordens.

Die Alster und der Nieselregen – das war's allerdings noch lange nicht mit den Hamburger Gewässern. Der Wohlstand der Stadt verdankt sich in erster Linie den Fluten der Elbe, Lebens- und Hauptschlagader der pulsierenden Metropole. In zweiter Linie verdankt er sich dem kreativen Umgang der Stadtoberen mit dem Recht. Ein gefälschter Freibrief Kaiser Barbarossas erlaubte ab 1189 den Hamburgern den zollfreien Warenverkehr auf der Unterelbe bis zur Nordsee. Rund 300 Jahre später stellte eine ebenso dreist manipulierte Landkarte die Norderelbe als Hauptarm des Stroms dar, wodurch Hamburg – auch dies zum Ärger der Nachbarstädte – weiterhin die lukrativen Schiffszölle der übrigen Seefahrer abgreifen konnte.

Einen nicht gekannten Aufschwung erlebte die Stadt ab dem 13. Jahrhundert durch die europäische Vernetzung ihrer Kaufleute im Wirtschaftsverbund der Hanse. Seehandelsrouten aus Skandinavien, dem nördlichen Osteuropa und dem Süden des Kontinents

of millionaires and convertibles in Germany, but also enjoys a reputation as a city of benefactors and patrons. All go in for casual understatement. Not for nothing are Wellington boots the high heels of the North.

The Alster and drizzly rain are far from everything that links Hamburg with water. The city owes its affluence primarily to the waters of the River Elbe, the lifeblood and main artery of this vibrant metropolis. Secondly, it owes its existence to the city fathers' creative ways with the law. A forged charter from Emperor Frederick Barbarossa in 1189 allowed Hamburgers to transport goods duty-free on the lower reaches of the Elbe as far as the North Sea. Around 300 years later an equally brazenly manipulated map portrayed the Norderelbe (Northern Elbe) as the main branch of the river. As a result Hamburg – again to the annoyance of neighbouring towns – was able to continue collecting lucrative customs duties from other seafarers.

From the thirteenth century, the city experienced an unprecedented boom when it joined the Hanseatic League, bringing its merchants into a network of European cities. Sea-trade routes from Scandinavia, northeast, and southern Europe came together in Hamburg

Der Hamburger „Michel“ von der Elbe aus gesehen. 453 Stufen führen hinauf auf den Turm der bedeutendsten Barockkirche Norddeutschlands, nach einem Brand 1912 wieder aufgebaut.

Von der Aussichtsplattform des Hamburg-Wahrzeichens genießt man einen herrlichen Ausblick über Alster, Elbe und den Hafen. Für Couch Potatoes gibt es einen Aufzug.

Hamburg's “Michel” seen from the Elbe. Four hundred and fifty three steps lead up the tower of North Germany's most important Baroque church, which was rebuilt after a fire in 1912.

From the viewing platform of this Hamburg landmark you have a superb view of the Alster, the Elbe and the port. Couch potatoes may take the elevator.

Königlicher Besuch am Kreuzfahrtterminal in der HafenCity. Bestaunt vom Treppenpublikum vor dem Unilever-Haus hat der britische Luxusliner *Queen Mary 2* festgemacht, eine immer wieder gern gesehene Lady im Hamburger Hafen – und eine Schau für sich, wenn sie zum Überholen bei Blohm + Voss ins Trockendock manövriert wird.

A royal visitor to the HafenCity cruise terminal. Onlookers on the steps outside the Unilever building gaze in wonder as the British luxury liner *Queen Mary 2* moors. She is always welcome in the port of Hamburg, and watching her being manoeuvred into the Blohm + Voss dry dock for an overhaul is a sight in itself.

Historie trifft Zukunft: In der Deichstraße am Nikolaifleet liegen die ältesten Bürgerhäuser Hamburgs. Dem Großen Brand von 1842 entgangen, vereinten sie Wohnen, Kontor und Speicher unter einem Dach. Dahinter der neue kulturelle Leuchtturm der Stadt: die 2017 eingeweihte Elbphilharmonie, von den Hamburgern kumpelig „Elphi“ genannt.

History meets future: Hamburg's oldest town houses are in Deichstrasse on the Nikolaifleet canal. These buildings, which survived the Great Fire of 1842, combined living, office and storage space under one roof. Behind them the city's new cultural landmark, the Elbphilharmonie concert hall. Inaugurated in 2017, Hamburgers have given it the chummy nickname "Elphi."

An den Landungsbrücken starten nicht nur die Hafenrundfahrten, sie sind auch „Haltestelle“ für den ganz normalen Fahrgastverkehr auf der Elbe, ob Richtung „Elphi“, zu den Musical-Hallen gegenüber oder elbabwärts zu den Obstanbaugebieten im Alten Land. Der grün bemützte Pegelturm zeigt an, wie es um die Elbfluten steht.

The Landungsbrücken landing stages are not only the starting point for sightseeing boat tours of the port, but also a stopping point for ordinary passenger ferries that ply on the Elbe, whether in the direction of “Elphi,” to the musical venues across the river, or downstream to the Altes Land orchard region. The green-capped gauge tower shows the water level of the Elbe.

trafen sich in Hamburg und machten es zu *dem* Verkehrsknotenpunkt im Norden. Der Import-Boom der Gründerjahre ab 1871 sowie die Weiterverarbeitung der kolonialen Güter im Freihafen rund um die 1888 eröffnete Speicherstadt bescherten Deutschlands „Tor zur Welt“ eine weitere Blütezeit und ließen es zum größten Seehafen des Landes werden. Zwar sind es noch fast hundert Kilometer bis zum offenen Meer, doch gerade die Binnenlage mit ihrer Anbindung ans Schienennetz macht Hamburg bis heute als Handelsstandort so attraktiv.

Ein Zehntel des Stadtgebiets nimmt der Hafen ein. Mit seinen vier Container- und drei Kreuzfahrtterminals ist er Taktgeber und ökonomisches Herzstück der Stadt. Vom Geestrücken an seiner Nordseite, Hinterlassenschaft der letzten Eiszeit, bieten sich Ausblicke über eine beeindruckende Industrie-Silhouette der maritimen Art. Die Giganten der Meere liegen hoch und trocken bei Blohm + Voss in den Docks. Gewaltige Hafenkräne nicken von den Containerterminals herüber und bilden den geschäftigen Hintergrund für die Hamburger Veteranen der Seefahrt an den Landungsbrücken: Das ehemalige Segelschulschiff

and made it *the* transport hub in the North. The import boom during the Wilhelminian period from 1871 and the further processing of colonial goods in the Speicherstadt, or Warehouse City, free port opened in 1888, bestowed another period of prosperity on Germany’s “Gateway to the World” and turned it into the country’s largest seaport. True, Hamburg is nearly one hundred kilometres from the open sea, but it is precisely this inland location with its connection to the railway network that makes the city so attractive as a location for trade to this day.

The port covers one tenth of the urban area. With its four container and three cruise liner terminals it is the pacemaker and economic heart of the city. From the elevated geest ridge along its north bank, a relic of the last Ice Age, one has views of an impressive silhouette of maritime industry. Gigantic vessels lie high and dry in the Blohm + Voss docks. Enormous port cranes nod across from the container terminals, forming a bustling backdrop to Hamburg’s seafaring veterans by the Landungsbrücken landing stages. The *Rickmer Rickmers,* a sailing ship formerly used for training, is berthed there, along with the elegant South America

Schiffsveteranen in der HafenCity, Hamburgs jüngstem Stadtteil. Am Schwimmponton des neuen Traditionsschiffhafens begegnen sich historische Segler und Dampfschifffahrt. Links im Bild die *Schaarhörn,* die ab 1908 als Staatsyacht Kaiser Wilhelm II. durch den Hafen schippern sollte – und nebenbei die Elbe vermessen. Nur Letzteres hat geklappt.

Vintage boats in the HafenCity, Hamburg's newest district. Historic sailing vessels and steam shipping meet by the floating pontoon in this new traditional port. On the left is the *Schaarhörn,* built in 1908 as Hamburg's state yacht. The plan was for her to sail Kaiser Wilhelm II through the port, measuring the depth of the Elbe as she did. Only the latter worked out in the end.

In der HafenCity stapeln sich die „Bauklötzchen“ internationaler Stararchitekten. Von links oben im Uhrzeigersinn: Marco-Polo-Terrassen am Grasbrookhafen mit Blick auf den Dalmannkai, der gläserne Kubus des *Spiegel*-Verlagshauses, die Haltestelle „HafenCity Universität“ der neuen U-Bahn-Linie 4, direkt am Elbufer die Firmenzentrale von Unilever.

The HafenCity has a lot of “building blocks” by international star architects. Clockwise from top left: the Marco-Polo-Terrassen at Grasbrookhafen with a view of the Dalmannkai quay, the glass cube of the *Spiegel* publishing house, the HafenCity University station on the new underground line 4, and standing right on the bank of the Elbe the Unilever headquarters.

Das gläserne Wellengebirge der Elbphilharmonie, errichtet auf dem roten Klinkersockel des ehemaligen Kaispeichers A, überragt die Highlights der Stadt. Zu ihren Füßen die elegante *Cap San Diego*, heute Museumsschiff. Links im Bild das Hanseatic Trade Center.

The Elbphilharmonie, a wavy glass mountain built on the red clinker brick base of former quayside Warehouse A, towers above the city's other highlights. At its feet is the elegant *Cap San Diego*, which is now a museum ship. On the left of the picture is the Hanseatic Trade Center.

CAP SAN DIEGO

Rickmer Rickmers liegt hier und der elegante Südamerikafrachter *Cap San Diego* von 1961. Von New York kehrt nach vielen Jahren auch die *Peking* zurück in den Hamburger Hafen; die Viermastbark aus der legendären Baureihe der Flying-P-Liner der Hamburger Reederei F. Laeisz lief 1911 hier vom Stapel. 2020 soll ihre Restaurierung abgeschlossen sein, danach wird sie stolzes Wahrzeichen des neuen Hafenmuseums im Hansahafen. Auch ihr Jahrgangsgenosse, der Alte Elbtunnel, hat seine Wiederherstellung zur Hälfte hinter sich. Frisch geliftet erstrahlt bereits eine der beiden Röhren in neuem Glanz, die zweite soll ab 2019 folgen. Bei der Einweihung durch Kaiser Wilhelm II. war er die erste Flussunterquerung der Welt und eine technische Sensation.
Eine technische – und akustische – Sensation von heute ist nach knapp einem Jahrzehnt der Dissonanzen um ihren Bau die 2017 eröffnete Elbphilharmonie. In exponierter Lage von Hamburgs neuem Stadtteil, der HafenCity, ruht das Wellengebirge aus Glas auf dem roten Backsteinsockel des ehemaligen Kaispeichers A aus den 1960er-Jahren. Dort bereitet es all jenen einen funkelnden Empfang, die sich Hamburg von der Wasserseite nähern. Allen anderen natürlich auch.

freighter *Cap San Diego,* built in 1961. From New York is the *Peking* back in Hamburg. This four-master barque from the legendary Flying-P class of liners belonging to the Hamburg shipping company F. Laeisz was launched here in 1911. Its restoration is due for completion in 2020; it will then be the proud landmark of the new Port Museum in the Hansahafen. The restoration of its contemporary, the Alter Elbtunnel (Old Elbe Tunnel), is also half completed; after a makeover, one of its two tubes has regained its former splendour, while the other is due for completion from 2019 on. When inaugurated by Kaiser Wilhelm II, this was the world's first underwater river crossing and a technical sensation.
A modern technical, and acoustic, sensation is the Elbphilharmonie, which was opened in 2017 after almost a decade of discord over its building. In a prominent location in Hamburg's new district, the HafenCity, this undulating mountain of glass stands on the red-brick base of a 1960s building, the former Quay Warehouse A. There it gives a sparkling reception to everyone approaching Hamburg by water, and of course everyone else.

Hafenimpressionen von über- bis unterirdisch. Von links oben im Uhrzeigersinn: Der Pegelturm an den Landungsbrücken wacht im Abendlicht über die *Queen Mary 2,* die Museumsschiffe *Cap San Diego* und *Rickmer Rickmers,* der frisch renovierte Alte Elbtunnel, 1911 erste Flussunterquerung Europas und eine technische Sensation.

Impressions of the port. Clockwise from top left: in the evening light the gauge tower by the Landungsbrücken keeps watch on the *Queen Mary 2,* the museum ships *Cap San Diego* and *Rickmer Rickmers,* the freshly renovated Alter Elbtunnel (Old Elbe Tunnel), Europe's first-ever tunnel under a river and a technical sensation when it was opened in 1911.

Hamburg besitzt den drittgrößten Containerhafen Europas, Umschlag knapp zehn Millionen Standardcontainer im Jahr. Nicht mehr als drei Minuten benötigt ein Kranführer für das Bergen eines Containers aus dem Schiffsbauch. Ein Präzisionsjob in schwindelnder Höhe, Nervenkitzel inklusive.

Hamburg has Europe's third-largest container port, which handles nearly ten million standard containers per year. A crane driver takes no more than three minutes to retrieve a container from the belly of a vessel. A precision job at dizzying heights, thrills included.

Keine Hafenrundfahrt ohne Riesenfrachter, blau-rote Containerbrücken und die wilden Hafengeschichten, die die Barkassenführer (auch „He lücht“, plattdeutsch für „Er lügt“, genannt) zum Besten geben. Bis zu 30 000 Euro kann das Hafengeld für übergroße Containerschiffe für einen Anlauf im Hamburger Hafen betragen. An einem Tag.

No tour of the harbour is complete without gigantic cargo vessels, blue and red gantry cranes that handle containers, and tall stories about the port told by launch captains – who are also known as “He lücht” (Low German dialect for “He’s lying.”) The port dues for megacontainer vessels in the port of Hamburg can be up to 30,000 euros – per day.

Mit zehn Liegeplätzen ist der Containerterminal Burchardkai der größte seiner Art im Hamburger Hafen. Auch wenn es aussieht, als stünde alles still am Abend: Die Kran-Giganten, die bei hochgerecktem Hals an stählerne Giraffen erinnern, sind rund um die Uhr aktiv. Über dem Hafen mit seinen vier Containerterminals liegt deshalb auch nachts stets ein orangefarbener Schimmer, erzeugt von Tausenden Industrieleuchten – weithin sichtbar und weit entfernt von romantischer Abendstimmung.

With ten berths, the Burchardkai container terminal is the largest of its kind in the Port of Hamburg. It might look as if everything has come to a standstill in the evening, but the gigantic cranes, resembling steel giraffes when their necks are raised, are in operation round the clock. That is why an orange glow always hangs over the port with its four container terminals, even at night. It is generated by thousands of industrial lamps which can be seen from afar and have nothing in common with a romantic evening mood.

TERMINAL BURCHARDKAI
TERMINAL BURCHARDKAI
TERMINAL BURCHARDKAI
TERMINAL BURCHARDKAI
TERMINAL BURCHARDKAI
HHLA
Hapag-Lloyd
GLASGOW EXPRESS
HAMBURG

Kontorhausviertel und Speicherstadt

Hamburg war immer Bürgerstadt, nie Residenz eines Landesfürsten. Im Hamburger Rat, seit 1860 Senat genannt, saßen nüchtern-pragmatisch denkende Kaufleute, die im Sinne geschäftlicher Interessen handelten. Entsprechend geradlinig und schnörkellos präsentiert sich die Handels- und Wirtschaftsmetropole bis heute: keine Schlösser und pompösen Alleen, keine kostspieligen royalen Spleens, kein goldverbrämter Kitsch oder gar Größenwahn.
Stattdessen steingewordene Gediegenheit allerorten – nicht nur rund um die Binnenalster, sondern vor allem in Form sachlicher Kontorhäuser (das bekannteste ist das Chilehaus von 1924) und einer giebel- und zinnengeschmückten Speicherstadt im roten Klinker-Look, beides seit 2015 Weltkulturerbe. Ein Wunder, dass sie überhaupt erhalten blieb, die historische Speicherstadt, denn wenn etwas den wirtschaftlichen Interessen im Weg steht in Hamburg, wird grundsätzlich nicht lange gefackelt. Kunstgeschichtliche oder architektonische Bedeutung hin oder her. Der bis 1248 erbaute Mariendom ist baufällig? Kein Problem für die Stadtoberen des frühen 19. Jahrhunderts: weg damit. Der Dovenhof von 1885/86, erstes Kontorhaus Hamburgs, erbaut von

Kontorhaus district and Speicherstadt

Hamburg was always a civil city, never the seat of a prince. The Hamburg Council, renamed the Senate in 1860, was made up of coolheaded, pragmatically minded merchants who acted in the interests of business. This trading and economic metropolis presents a correspondingly solid, unadorned image to this day – no palaces or grandiose boulevards, no costly royal follies, no gold-trimmed kitsch or indeed megalomania.
Instead, everywhere you look, solidity in bricks and mortar, not only around the Binnenalster (Inner Alster), but above all in the form of sober office buildings, the best known of which is the Chilehaus built in 1924, and the red clinker brick Speicherstadt, or Warehouse City, adorned with gables and pinnacles. Both have been World Heritage sites since 2015. That the historic Warehouse City survived at all is a miracle, because basically in Hamburg if something stands in the way of business interests not a great deal of dithering takes place, regardless of art historical or architectural significance. So St Mary's Cathedral, completed in 1248, was in a state of disrepair? The early nineteenth-century city fathers had no problem in getting rid of it. The French Renaissance-style Dovenhof, Hamburg's first

Ein Ozeanliner an Land, grandios gestrandet im historischen Kontorhausviertel: das Chilehaus von 1924. Filigrane Backsteinarchitektur mit elegant geschwungenen Linien macht es zum Flaggschiff und berühmtesten Kontorhaus der Stadt. Seinem Erbauer Fritz Höger trug es den Namen „Klinker-Sticker“ ein.

The Chilehaus, built in 1924, resembles an ocean liner on dry land, magnificently stranded in the historic Kontorhaus district. Intricate brick architecture and elegant curved lines make it a flagship and the city’s most famous office building. It earned its architect Fritz Höger the nickname “Klinker-Sticker.”

Weltkulturerbe im Klinker-Look: die historische Speicherstadt mit ihren roten Zinnen und Giebeln. Ab 1883 auf zwei Inseln sowie Millionen von Eichenpfählen errichtet, ist sie der größte Lagerhauskomplex der Welt. Wo einst die Windenwärter wohnten, am Zusammenfluss zweier Fleete, behauptet das *Wasserschlösschen* an der Dienerreihe seinen Platz.

World Heritage in clinker brick: the historic Speicherstadt (Warehouse City) with its red pinnacles and gables. Built from 1883 on two islands and millions of oak piles, it is the world's largest warehouse complex. The idyllic *Wasserschlösschen,* where the winch keepers used to live, guards its position at the confluence of two canals on Dienerreihe.

Roter Backstein nicht nur für die Fassaden. Noch gibt es das eine oder andere Tee- oder Kaffeekontor, während „fliegende Teppiche“ ihren Weg in den Speicher per Seilwinde antreten. Rechts das *Internationale Maritime Museum* im Kaispeicher B.

Redbrick is not only for facades. The odd tea or coffee trading business still survives, while “flying carpets” make their way into the warehouse by cable winch. On the right is the *International Maritime Museum* in quayside Warehouse B.

Während in früheren Zeiten Kaffee-, Tee- und Gewürzdüfte durch die Fleete des Freihafens waberten, beherbergen die ehemaligen Speicher heute verschiedene Museen sowie die größte Modelleisenbahn der Welt. Hinter dieser Fassade im typischen Rotklinker verbirgt sich die Hamburg Port Authority, das Management des Hamburger Hafens.

In former times, the aromas of coffee, tea and spices wafted through the freeport canals. Now the former warehouses accommodate various museums and the world's biggest model railway. Behind this façade in typical red clinker brick is the Hamburg Port Authority, which manages the Port of Hamburg.

Eine Bootstour durch die Backsteinschluchten der Speicherstadt sorgt immer wieder für Gänsehautmomente. Am linken Bildrand lugt der Rathausturm hervor. Sein Pendant im Stil der niederländischen Renaissance findet er im Uhrenturm des Gebäudes der Hamburger Hafen und Logistik AG (HHLA) gleich daneben, auch „Rathaus der Speicherstadt“ genannt.

A boat trip through the red-brick ravines of the Speicherstadt is always good for some spine-tingling sights. On the far left of the picture, the Rathaus tower peeps out. Its counterpart in Dutch Renaissance style, just to the right of it, is the clock tower of Hamburger Hafen und Logistik AG (HHLA), also known as the "Speicherstadt City Hall."

Der weiße Kubus der Galerie der Gegenwart von Architekt Mathias Ungers bildet seit 1996 ein optisches Gegengewicht zu den beiden älteren Gebäuden der Hamburger Kunsthalle. Auf einer ehemaligen Bastion der Hamburger Wallanlagen zwischen Binnen- und Außenalster gelegen, komplettiert er die acht Jahrhunderte umfassenden Sammlungen.

Since 1996 the white cube of the Galerie der Gegenwart contemporary art gallery by architect Mathias Ungers has provided a visual counterweight to the two older buildings of the Hamburg Kunsthalle. Built on a former bastion of the Hamburg ramparts between Binnenalster and Aussenalster, it brings collections covering eight centuries right up to date.

Martin Haller im Stil der französischen Renaissance, steht dort, wo 1967 der Produzent eines großen deutschen Nachrichtenmagazins seine künftige verlegerische Heimstatt sieht? Muss er eben Platz machen.
Bereits im Jahr 1888 trug dieser spezifische Umgang mit kulturellen Werten der Hansestadt das Etikett „Freie und Abrissstadt Hamburg“ ein. Alfred Lichtwark, ab 1886 legendärer Leiter der Hamburger Kunsthalle, hat es geprägt – damals im Hinblick auf den Abbruch eines dicht besiedelten Wohnviertels auf den Elbinseln Kehrwieder und Wandrahm. Und zwar für eben jene Speicherstadt aus rotem Backstein, die heute als weltweit einzigartig gilt.
Den traditionellen roten Klinker bevorzugte Anfang des 20. Jahrhunderts auch Architekt, Stadtplaner und Reformer Fritz Schumacher. Seine Bauten, von der berühmten Davidwache an der Reeperbahn bis zum Tropeninstitut, der Finanzbehörde am Gänsemarkt, dem Museum für Hamburgische Geschichte und den Gebäuden des Stadtparks, prägen trotz der Zerstörungen im Zweiten Weltkrieg bis heute maßgeblich das Gesicht der Stadt. Auch im öffentlichen und privaten Wohnungsbau ist der rote Klinker ein Klassiker. Begehrtes

Kontorhaus (office building), erected in 1885/86 by Martin Haller, stood on a site that in 1967 the producer of a major German news magazine saw as his future publishing headquarters? Well, it just had to make way.
Already back in 1888 this particular way of dealing with cultural assets earned Hamburg the nickname “Free and Demolition City” (a play on its actual name Free and Hanseatic City). This epithet was coined by Alfred Lichtwark, from 1886 the legendary director of the Hamburg Kunsthalle art gallery. At the time he was referring to the demolition of a densely populated residential district on the Elbe islands of Kehrwieder and Wandrahm, in fact to make way for that very same Speicherstadt, the ensemble of redbrick port warehouses now regarded as unique in the world.
The early twentieth-century architect, town planner and reformer Fritz Schumacher also favoured traditional red clinker brick. Despite the destruction of World War II, his buildings, ranging from the famous Davidwache police station on the Reeperbahn to the Institute for Tropical Medicine, the Tax Authority on Gänsemarkt, the Museum for Hamburg History and the buildings in the Stadtpark municipal park still play

Und immer wieder der rote Backstein, Lieblingsbaustoff auch des ehemaligen Oberbaudirektors Fritz Schumacher (1869–1947). Links oben die Eingangshalle des Museums für Hamburgische Geschichte. Darunter ein Klinkerdetail der Finanzbehörde am Gänsemarkt, rechts das Treppenhaus der Hamburger Handwerkskammer am Holstenwall.

Time and again redbrick, the favourite building material of Fritz Schumacher (1869–1947), once the city's director of building. Top left is the entrance hall of the Museum for Hamburg History. Below is a detailed image of brickwork at the tax authority building on Gänsemarkt, and on the right the staircase of the Hamburg Chamber of Trade on Holstenwall.

1916 fertiggestellt und 2017 nach Modernisierung wiedereröffnet: das Planetarium im Winterhuder Stadtpark. Konzipiert als Wasserturm, bildete der elegante Art-Déco-Bau nach einem Entwurf des Dresdner Architekten Oscar Menzel das architektonische Gegengewicht zur im Zweiten Weltkrieg zerstörten und nicht wieder aufgebauten Stadthalle.

Completed in 1916 and reopened in 2017 after modernisation: the Planetarium in the Stadtpark (Municipal Park) in Winterhude. This elegant Art Déco building was erected to a design by Dresden architect Oscar Menzel and was originally conceived as a water tower. It is the architectural counterweight to a civic hall that was destroyed in World War II and not rebuilt.

Wohnobjekt ist nach wie vor die sogenannte Hamburger Kaffeemühle. Die hat nichts mit braunen Bohnen zu tun, sondern beschreibt die würfelförmigen Villen mit den weißen Sprossenfenstern aus den 1920er- und 30er- Jahren, die die Zeitgenossen an eine Kaffeemühle erinnerten. Großbürgerliches Wohnen fand jedoch nicht nur in Rot statt. Nach wie vor bauliches Aushängeschild der Stadt sind die weißen Villen an Alster und Elbe, im feinen Harvestehude ebenso wie an Hamburgs Prachtstraße im Westen, der Elbchaussee.

a defining role in the city's image. Red clinker brick is also a classic material for public and private residences. A still sought-after style of residential property is known as a "Hamburg coffee grinder." The name has nothing to do with brown beans, but describes the cube-shaped mansions with white glazing bars in their windows that were built in the 1920s and 1930s and in those days reminded people of coffee mills. However, the grand bourgeois lifestyle was not only lived in red. The white mansions beside Alster and Elbe in elegant Harvestehude and along Elbchaussee, Hamburg's grand boulevard in the west, are still an architectural Hamburg showpiece.

Villenarchitektur in Weiß-Rot am noblen Leinpfad an der Alster. Von Bord eines Alsterschiffs lassen sich großbürgerliches Wohnen und grüne Idylle mitten in der Stadt bestaunen. Und ein bisschen auch beneiden.

Mansion architecture in white and red on upscale Leinpfad alongside the Alster. From the deck of an Alster boat one can marvel at upper class living and green idylls in the middle of the city. And perhaps feel a little envious.

Wo Hamburg am jüngsten ist – von St. Georg bis Ottensen

Nun ist es keineswegs so, dass vor lauter Gediegenheit in der Hansestadt niemand unter 50 wäre. Weit gefehlt. Hamburg besitzt zahlreiche boomende Hochschulen und Universitäten, gilt als Hochburg der Medien- und Werbeindustrie und hat eine hochproduktive und -aktive Musikszene. Hamburg ist jung oder fühlt sich so, davon zeugen die vielen quirligen Viertel mit Bars, Musikclubs, Restaurants, Galerien und individuellen Geschäften jenseits von Prada, Gucci & Co. Tag- und Nachtschwärmer sind hier die am weitesten verbreitete Spezies – und Multikulti ist der ganz normale Aggregatzustand.

St. Georg, einst verrufener Stadtteil zwischen südöstlichem Alsterufer und Hamburger Hauptbahnhof, hat sein Image deutlich aufpoliert in den vergangenen 25 Jahren. Heute steht das Viertel für urbane Lebensart, großstädtisches Publikum und schicke Altbauwohnungen an Kopfsteinpflaster. Die einstigen Spelunken haben sich in cool-relaxte Cafés verwandelt, in Restaurants, Clubs und einschlägige Bars, befördert durch das kreative Potenzial der hier heimisch gewordenen Schwulenszene. Auch das *Deutsche Schauspielhaus,* größtes Sprechtheater des Landes, hat in

Where Hamburg is youngest – from St. Georg to Ottensen

It is by no means true that the Hanseatic city is so solid and sedate that nobody under the age of 50 lives there. That is far off the mark. Hamburg has a large number of booming universities and colleges, is regarded as a stronghold of the media and advertising industry and boasts a highly productive and energetic musical scene. Hamburg is young or feels so, as is visible in its many lively neighbourhoods with bars, music clubs, restaurants, galleries and individual shops a world away from Prada, Gucci and the like. Here, day and night owls are the most common species, and multiculturalism is the absolutely normal physical state.

St. Georg, once a disreputable district between the southeast bank of the Alster and Hamburg central station, has polished its image considerably in the last twenty-five years. Now the quarter epitomizes urbane lifestyle, with its metropolitan public and chic apartments in old buildings on cobbled streets. Erstwhile dives have been transformed into cool, relaxed cafés, into restaurants, clubs and trendy bars, encouraged by the creative potential of the gay scene that has become indigenous here. Moreover, the *Deutsches Schauspielhaus,* the federal state's largest theatre of the spoken

1909 als Grand Hotel für die Erste-Klasse-Passagiere der Hamburg-Amerika-Linie eröffnet: das Hotel *Atlantic* mit weißer Gründerzeitfassade und Weltkugel. Udo Lindenberg ist Stammgast. Dazu der Blick über St. Georg mit Hauptbahnhof und *Deutschem Schauspielhaus*. Seit 170 Jahren ein Original der Hamburger Kneipenszene: das *Nagel* an der Kirchenallee.

The Hotel *Atlantic* with its white Wilhelminian-era facade and rooftop globe was built in 1909 as a grand hotel for first-class passengers of the Hamburg-America Line shipping company. Then there is the view over the St. Georg area with the Central Station and the *Deutsches Schauspielhaus* theatre. *Nagel* has been a hallmark of the Hamburg pub scene for 170 years.

Am Spielbudenplatz an der Reeperbahn in St. Pauli steppt nicht nur der Bär, da tanzen sogar die Türme und bieten von der *Heaven's Bar* in luftiger Höhe eine grandiose Aussicht über den Hafen und die HafenCity.

Overlooking the buzz of groovy Spielbudenplatz on the Reeperbahn in St. Pauli are the high-rise "Dancing Towers." *Heaven's Bar* in the airy heights has a superb view of the port and the HafenCity.

Die von den aufmüpfigen Anwohnern erkämpfte Grünanlage *Park Fiction* am Geesthang von St. Pauli. Im Gewölbe einer alten Eisengießerei genießt man die Sushi-Spezialitäten des glamourösen Design-Hotels *East*. Am Abend: Showtime auf der sündigen Meile – von Musicaltheater bis Table Dance.

Rebellious residents campaigned to secure the *Park Fiction* green space on the geest slope in St. Pauli. In the vault of an old iron foundry, diners now savour sushi specialities served by glamorous designer hotel *East*. In the evening: showtime on the "wicked mile" – from musical theatre to table dancing.

In schwungvollem Bogen spannt sich seit 1974 die zweitlängste Straßenbrücke Deutschlands über den Köhlbrand, einen Seitenarm der Süderelbe.

Since 1974 Germany's second-longest road bridge has crossed the Köhlbrand, a tributary of the Süderelbe, in a sweeping curve.

Die Reeperbahn, Hamburgs sexy Meile. Von links oben im Uhrzeigersinn: Tür an Tür – *St. Pauli Theater* und Davidwache, Europas kleinstes Polizeirevier, der rot-plüschige Zuschauerraum des *St. Pauli Theaters*, die Große Freiheit mit ihren Clubs und die Konkurrenz von um die Ecke an der Reeperbahn.

The Reeperbahn, Hamburg's sexy mile. Clockwise from top left: Near neighbours: *St. Pauli Theater* and the Davidwache, Europe's smallest police station, the red plush auditorium of *St. Pauli Theater*, Grosse Freiheit with its clubs, and competition from the Reeperbahn around the corner.

Wo Hamburg am jüngsten ist – von St. Georg bis Ottensen

St. Georg, an der Kirchenallee, seine repräsentative Spielstätte.
St. Pauli. Der Mix ist es, der diesen Kiez an der Elbe ausmacht. Bürgerliche Kultur trifft auf eine ausgeprägte Club- und Kneipenszene, Rotlicht auf Touristen und Partyvolk auf Teenies mit ihrer ersten Wodkaflasche unterm Arm. Fast immer ausgebuchte Klassiker sind, gleich neben der Davidwache an der Reeperbahn, das denkmalgeschützte *St. Pauli Theater*, das *Schmidt Theater* und *Schmidts Tivoli* mit seinen Ablegern sowie das *Operettenhaus*, Hamburgs erstes Musicaltheater. Mittendrin und gern hinter der ersten Reihe leben die ganz normalen St. Paulianer. Etwas mehr Ruhe wünschen sie sich gelegentlich in ihrem geliebten Viertel, wo es durchaus auch romantisch zugeht. Lieblingsort, den man dort nicht vermutet hätte: der Hein-Köllisch-Platz mit seinen Gründerzeitfassaden, den rundgetretenen Pflastersteinen, gemütlichen Restaurants und den im Frühling üppig blühenden Kirschbäumen.
Als aufmüpfigste Stadtteile Hamburgs gelten die Schanze und das Karoviertel, versinnbildlicht durch die *Rote Flora*, selbstverwaltetes Kultur- und Stadtteilzentrum mit Krawall-Image. Wenn's kracht in der Stadt,

Where Hamburg is youngest – from St. Georg to Ottensen

word, has its showpiece building on Kirchenallee in St. Georg.
And then St. Pauli. The mix is what makes this neighbourhood by the Elbe, a mix of bourgeois culture and a distinctive club and pub scene, red light establishments and tourists, partygoers and teenagers with their first bottle of vodka under their arms. Classic venues close to the Davidwache on the Reeperbahn, such as *St. Pauli Theater* (now a protected historic monument), the *Schmidt Theater* and *Schmidts Tivoli* with its offshoots, are almost always fully booked, as is the *Operettenhaus*, Hamburg's first musical theatre. Amidst all this, and for preference away from the main drag, perfectly ordinary St. Pauli residents go about their lives. Sometimes they wish for a little more peace and quiet in their beloved neighbourhood, which is certainly not without romance. A favourite place you would never have suspected was there is Hein-Köllisch-Platz with its Wilhelminian facades, worn cobblestones, cosy restaurants and lush cherry-tree blossom in spring.
Generally seen as Hamburg's most rebellious districts are Schanze and the Karoviertel, symbolised by the *Rote Flora*, a self-managed cultural and neighbourhood

Ganz ohne Wasserwerfer, dafür mit Laisser-faire bis zur Bordsteinkante: die Schanze am Schulterblatt. Gleich um die Ecke bei der Alten Rinderschlachthalle, die Flohschanze, trubeliger Multikulti-Flohmarkt am Sonnabend. (Apropos: Am „Sonnabend“ erkennt man den Hamburger. „Samstag“ geht gar nicht.)

No water cannon here, just laissez-faire to the edge of the pavement: the Schanze on Schulterblatt. Just round the corner at the old abattoir is the Flohschanze, a bustling multicultural Saturday flea market. (Note: Someone who calls Saturday “Sonnabend” is recognizably a Hamburger. “Samstag” won’t do at all.)

Zwischen Kölsch und Tequila vor *Oma's Apotheke*, wo die Bierbänke bis zur Straße reichen. Dito beim Sardinas- und Paella-Schlemmen beim Portugiesen. Als Open-Air-Galerie versteht sich das gesamte Schanzenviertel; Street Art vom Feinsten gibt's am laufenden Meter.

Amongst Kölsch beer and tequila outside *Oma's Apotheke*, where the beer benches extend to the street. The same goes when feasting on sardines and paella at a Portuguese restaurant. The entire Schanzenviertel neighbourhood sees itself as an open-air gallery, with finest street art on show by the metre.

dann da, in unmittelbarer Nähe zum Messezentrum – brennende Barrikaden und Wasserwerfer inklusive. Wenn's gerade nicht kracht, ist die Schanze dank Gentrifizierung mittlerweile kreuzbrav, ein angesagter Treffpunkt für Studenten, Werbevolk, Partygänger und Modebegeisterte auf der Suche nach Ausgefallenem – obwohl das Ausgefallene hier schon wieder Mainstream ist. Der Gott des Konsums hat Einzug gehalten ins ehemals preiswerte Altbauviertel, junge Familien ebenso, und der Raum für freakigere Lebensentwürfe in der Stadt ist wieder mal einen Tick geschrumpft.

Konsum der kulinarischen Art ist das Stichwort im Portugiesenviertel. Zwischen den St. Pauli-Landungsbrücken, Ausgangspunkt für die beliebten Hafenrundfahrten, und Hamburgs göttlichstem Wahrzeichen St. Michaelis – der bedeutendsten Barockkirche Norddeutschlands, Kosename „Michel“ – stößt mediterrane Küche und Wesensart auf Hamburger Geschmacksnerven. Die portugiesisch-spanisch geprägte Restaurantszene mit ihrem munteren Nachtleben provoziert Mittelmeergefühle an der Elbe. An lauen Sommerabenden werden die Fenster weit aufgerissen, die Tische wandern auf die Bürgersteige, drinnen läuft in wenigstens

centre with a rowdy image. When trouble flares up in the city, it is there in the immediate vicinity of the Messezentrum exhibition halls – including burning barricades and water cannons. In quieter times, thanks to gentrification the Schanze is as good as gold, and a popular meeting place for students, advertising folk, partygoers and fashionistas on the lookout for something unusual – although here the unusual is now the norm. However, the god of consumerism has entered this once low-cost neighbourhood of old buildings, as have young families, and the space for more offbeat ways of living in the city has shrunk a little further.

Consumerism of a culinary nature is the watchword in the Portuguese quarter. In the area between the St. Pauli-Landungsbrücken, the starting point for popular harbour boat trips, and Hamburg's foremost sacred landmark St. Michael's Church, commonly known as the Michel and the most distinguished Baroque church in northern Germany, Mediterranean cuisine meets Hamburg taste-buds. The Portuguese and Spanish-dominated restaurant scene with its lively nightlife awakens Mediterranean feelings on the Elbe. On mild summer evenings, windows are thrown open wide and

Kleinbürgerlich bis zu Omas Blümchenservice mit Spitzendeckchen geht es in den *Krameramtsstuben* zu. Wenige Schritte unterhalb des „Michel“ hat sich Hamburgs letzte geschlossene Hofbebauung des 17. Jahrhunderts erhalten. Dicht an dicht fanden in den Fachwerkhäusern die Witwen der örtlichen Kleinhändler („Kramer“) eine Bleibe.

Details such as granny's flowered teaset and lace tablecloths set the lower middle-class tone in the *Krameramtsstuben*. A few steps down from the "Michel," Hamburg's last seventeenth-century self-contained courtyard complex has survived. The widows of local shopkeepers lived cheek by jowl in these half-timbered buildings.

Verwunschen und voller Melancholie schlummert der Jüdische Friedhof (1616–1877) mit seinen fast 9000 Grabsteinen von sephardischen und aschkenasischen Juden im Großstadtgetriebe der Königstraße in Altona. Er ist eines der weltweit bedeutendsten jüdischen Gräberfelder.

Enchanted and filled with melancholy, the Jewish Cemetery (1616–1877) with its nearly 9,000 gravestones of Sephardic and Ashkenazi Jews slumbers amid the metropolitan hustle and bustle of Königstrasse in Altona. It is one of the world's most important Jewish burial grounds.

zwei von vier Ecken Fußball auf dem Bildschirm, und draußen schreit Mama mit Inbrunst nach Pedro oder Luís. Während sich selbst der steife Hanseat ein bisschen fühlen darf wie Don Juan.
Seit 500 Jahren schon sind Portugiesen und Spanier in Hamburg ansässig. Damals kamen aus dem Süden wohlhabende jüdische Kaufleute, Ärzte und Rabbiner auf der Flucht vor religiöser Verfolgung durch die Inquisition. Ihnen verdankt Hamburg den Jüdischen Friedhof in Altona, einen verwunschenen Ort mit geradezu magischer Aura, auch er womöglich auf dem Weg zum Status eines Weltkulturerbes.
Das Flair von gestern weht durchs labyrinthische Ottensen, westlichstes der szenigen Stadtviertel. Doch auch dieser Kiez, zwischen Altonaer Bahnhof und dem hohen Elbufer gelegen, ist dabei sich aufzurüschen. Lange ein Bauern- und Handwerkerdorf, fiel er im 19. Jahrhundert der Industrialisierung anheim. 150 Jahre später lebten dank preiswerten Wohnraums überwiegend Studenten und Migranten in den engen Straßen und kleinteiligen Gebäuden. Heute sind die schicken Lofts in den ehemaligen Werk- und Industriehallen und die Altbauwohnungen in den gepflasterten Hinter-

tables appear on the pavements. Inside, football is screened on TV in at least two out of four corners, while outside Mama shouts insistently for Pedro or Luís. Amidst all this, even a straight-laced Hanseatic citizen can feel a little like Don Juan.
Portuguese and Spaniards have resided in Hamburg for 500 years. In those days, wealthy Jewish merchants, doctors and rabbis fleeing religious persecution by the Inquisition arrived from the south. Hamburg owes to them the Jewish Cemetery in Altona, an enchanted place with an almost magical aura. It, too, may be on the way to gaining World Cultural Heritage status.
An air of times past wafts through labyrinthine Ottensen, the westernmost of the trendy city neighbourhoods. Yet even this neighbourhood between Altona railway station and the high bank of the Elbe is in the process of smartening itself up. For a long time a village of farmers and craftsmen, in the nineteenth century it fell victim to industrialization. A hundred and fifty years later, thanks to low-cost housing its narrow streets and small-scale buildings were inhabited mainly by students and migrants. Now, chic loft dwellings in former factory and industrial halls, and apartments in

höfen hochbegehrt von einem durchaus betuchten urbanen Publikum jeglichen Alters. Für lässig-entspannte Atmosphäre im Stadtteil sorgt der Mix aus kleinen Vintage-, Mode- und Wohndesignläden, buntem Marktgeschehen und Livemusik in einer ehemaligen Maschinenhalle, der legendären *Fabrik*. Sie gilt als erste Kultur- und Kommunikationsstätte Deutschlands, die aus einem Industriestandort hervorgegangen ist.

the cobbled back yards of old buildings are highly sought after by a well-to-do, urbane public of all ages. The district's casually relaxed atmosphere results from the mix of small vintage and fashion boutiques and design-for-living shops, colourful markets and live music in a former machine hall, the legendary *Fabrik*, regarded as the first cultural centre and meeting place in Germany to emerge from an industrial site.

So bunt wie lebendig: der quirlige Stadtteil Ottensen. Oben lässiges Publikum vor der *Filmhauskneipe* im ehemaligen Industriekomplex Zeisehallen, unten der Blumenmarkt in der Ottenser Hauptstraße. Als Denkmal der Industriegeschichte reckt rechts ein alter Lastkran den Hals vom Dach der *Fabrik*, Kulturzentrum seit den 1970er-Jahren.

Colourful and vivacious: the lively district of Ottensen. Above, laid-back drinkers and diners outside the *Filmhauskneipe* in the Zeisehallen former industrial complex, below the flower market in Ottenser Hauptstrasse. As a monument to industrial history, on the right an old crane stretches its neck from the roof of the *Fabrik*, a cultural centre since the 1970s.

Die Elbe – ein Lebensgefühl vom Fischmarkt bis Blankenese

Eine grüne Stadt ist Hamburg. Herrliche Parks lockern die steinerne Topografie auf, allen voran der große Stadtpark nördlich der Alster, wo Kunst und Freizeitkultur zu einem ganz besonderen Naherholungsgebiet verschmelzen. Auch längs der Elbe reiht sich, wie auf eine Perlenschnur gezogen, ein Landschaftspark an den anderen.

All das Grün aber vermag nichts daran zu ändern: Gefühlt liegt Hamburg am Meer. Nicht nur für Menschen aus südlicheren Gefilden, die die Landkarte womöglich nicht so richtig im Kopf haben, sondern auch für die Hamburger selbst.

Spätestens am Wochenende sind alle da, die auslüften, sich mal wieder den Wind um die Ohren wehen lassen wollen. Mit Kind und Kegel, mit Turbo-Buggy, Fahrrad oder Rollerskates. Mit Oma, wahlweise Hund, und es ist völlig egal, was das Wetter macht. Die Elbe sorgt für Frischluft im Kopf und für Horizont davor. Hier wird nicht flaniert wie an der Alster. Hier wird flott vorangeschritten. Die Elbe ist nicht nur Lebensader der Stadt. Die Elbe ist in Hamburg ein Lebensgefühl.

Überall, wo sie strömt, fließt oder träge ans Ufer schlappt, macht es sich breit. Rund um Deutschlands

The Elbe – an attitude to life from Fischmarkt to Blankenese

Hamburg is a green city. Superb parks relieve the stone topography, foremost among them the large Stadtpark municipal park north of the Alster, where arts and leisure cultures merge into a very special local recreational area. Meanwhile along the Elbe one landscaped park follows another like a string of pearls.

However, all this greenery does nothing to alter the fact that Hamburg feels like a city by the sea, not only to people from more southern parts who may not be well acquainted with the cartography, but also to Hamburgers themselves.

If not before, then certainly at weekends anyone wanting an airing and keen to feel the wind blowing round their ears again can be seen by the Elbe – with children, bag and baggage, with turbo pushchair, bicycle or roller-skates, with Granny and maybe a dog, no matter what the weather. The Elbe provides fresh air inside your head and a horizon before you. People here do not stroll as they do by the Alster. Instead, they step out energetically. The Elbe is not only the city's lifeline. In Hamburg, the Elbe is an attitude to life.

Wherever the river surges, flows or laps languidly by the bank this is evident, be it around Wilhelmsburg in

Ums frühe Aufstehen kommt nicht herum, wer am Sonntag den Hamburger Fischmarkt bei der ehemaligen Fischauktionshalle am Hafen besuchen möchte. Umso glücklicher geht man gegen zehn nach Hause – mit einer niederländischen Bananenpalme im Arm, einem lebendigen Perlhuhn oder dem toten Aal von Aale-Dieter.

If you want to visit the Hamburg Fish Market around the former fish auction hall by the port on Sunday morning, you have to get up early. You will be all the happier when you head for home at around 10 a.m. with a Dutch banana tree under your arm, a live guinea fowl or a dead eel from Dieter the eel man.

Hier sitzt man in der ersten Reihe und ganz dicht dran am Puls der Elbe. *Au Quai, Rive* oder schlicht *Fischereihafen Restaurant* heißen die Flaggschiffe der Edelgastronomie längs der Altonaer Fischmeile.

Here you have a front row seat and a finger on the pulse of the Elbe. *Au Quai, Rive* or plain *Fischereihafen Restaurant* are the names of fine dining flagships along the Altona fish mile.

Einen Steinwurf entfernt elbabwärts im Schlepperhafen von Neumühlen: die „Perlenkette“ der neuen Hafenbebauung. Die PS-starken Escort-Ladies der großen Pötte, die Schlepper, warten hier auf Containerriesen und Kreuzfahrtdampfer, die den Weg zu ihrem Liegeplatz nicht allein finden.

A stone's throw away down river in the Neumühlen tug port: the "string of pearls" of new buildings in the port area. In front of them, the powerful escort vessels, the tugs, wait for container giants and cruise liners unable to find their way to their berths alone.

Leuchtkristall mit Schiff-Appeal: der verwegene Bürokomplex *Dockland* von Hamburgs Stararchitekt Hadi Teherani an der Elbe beim Fischereihafen. Über zwei Freitreppen kann man dem Parallelogramm aus Glas und Stahl sogar aufs geneigte Dach steigen, vorausgesetzt, man ist schwindelfrei.

Luminous glass with the appeal of a ship: *Dockland*, a bold office complex designed by Hamburg's star architect Hadi Teherani, stands by the Elbe near the fishing port. You can even climb two open-air staircases to the inclined roof of this parallelogram of glass and steel – provided you do not suffer from vertigo.

größte Flussinsel Wilhelmsburg in Hamburg-Mitte ebenso wie Richtung Nordsee im Hamburger Westen. Zu den malerischsten Orten der Stadt zählen die ehemaligen Lotsen- und Fischerdörfer Övelgönne und Blankenese. Gleich hinterm Fischmarkt und dem ehemaligen Altonaer Fischereihafen, der mittlerweile zur angesagten Einkaufs- und Gastronomiemeile Große Elbstraße mutiert ist, geht's los.
Vorbei am Cruise Center Altona, am *Dockland*, dem schnittigen Glasgebilde von Stararchitekt Hadi Teherani, und am Schlepperhafen Neumühlen, wo die bulligen Kraftpakete auf Container- oder Kreuzfahrt-Kundschaft warten, führt der Weg zum Museumshafen in Övelgönne. Bewacht vom ehemaligen Pagensander Leuchtturm schaukeln historische Arbeitsschiffe auf den Wellen, flankiert von zahlreichen Restaurants und Freiluftcafés. Der Uferweg selbst: ein einziges Idyll. Gesäumt von ehemaligen Lotsen- und Kapitänshäusern in rotem Backstein sowie von glyzinienumrankten Wohngebäuden in weißer Seebad-Architektur blickt er über handtuchgroße Gärten Richtung Elbe. Romantikfaktor: zehn. Mindestens. Wäre da nicht der ewige Heavy-Metal-Sound des gegenüberliegenden Hafens,

central Hamburg, Germany's largest river island, or in the west of the city further toward the North Sea. The former river pilots' and fishing villages of Övelgönne and Blankenese are among the city's most picturesque places. Immediately behind the Fish Market and the former fishing port of Altona, which has now mutated into a popular shopping and gastronomy mile along Grosse Elbstrasse, is a good starting point.
Passing the Altona Cruise Center, past *Dockland*, the streamlined glass structure by star architect Hadi Teherani, and past Neumühlen tug harbour, where these sturdy little power packs wait for container or cruise ship clientele, you come to the Museumshafen (Museum Harbour) in Övelgönne. Guarded by the former Pagensand lighthouse, historic working vessels rock to and fro on the waves, flanked by numerous restaurants and cafés. The path along the riverbank is simply idyllic. Lined by redbrick houses that were formerly home to river pilots and captains and by wisteria-covered white residences in seaside architectural style, it opens vistas across handkerchief-sized gardens towards the Elbe. Romanticism score: ten. At least. Were it not for the ceaseless heavy metal sound from the port

Arbeitsschiffe aus zwei Jahrhunderten, zwischen 1880 und 1960 auf Kiel gelegt, dümpeln im Museumshafen in Övelgönne auf den graubraunen Fluten. Von der *Elbe 3*, dem ältesten seegängigen Feuerschiff der Welt, bis zum voll funktionstüchtigen Dampf-Eisbrecher *Stettin*, Jahrgang 1933.

Working vessels from two centuries whose keels were laid down between 1880 and 1960 bob up and down on the grey-brown water in Övelgönne Museum Harbour. They range from the *Elbe 3*, the world's oldest seagoing lightship, to the fully operational steam ice-breaker *Stettin*, built in 1933.

man wähnte sich zurückversetzt ins Dorfleben einer anderen Epoche.

Quasi mittendrin im Dorf Övelgönne beginnt das Strandleben, das zur Elbfolklore gehört wie das Rathaus zur Alster. Rummel- und Tummelplatz und eine Hamburger Ikone des lässigen Strandflairs ist die *Strandperle*. Eigentlich nur eine Bretterbude an hölzerner Terrasse, im Rücken die graffitiverzierte Backsteinmauer, ist der bessere Kiosk zu jeder Jahreszeit ein Anziehungspunkt für Liebhaber entspannten Outdoor-Genusses. Von ihrem Logenplatz am Wasser verfolgen sie interessiert das rege Treiben gegenüber am Containerhafen, auf der Elbe und am sandigen Ufer. Fünfzig Meter weiter oben verengt sich derweil die Fahrbahn der Elbchaussee zum Nadelöhr, weil kreativ geparkte Cabrios und Kombis den Straßenrand neu interpretieren.

Elbflair für Eingeweihte, mit etwas weniger Hipp und Hype, findet sich ein paar Kilometer flussabwärts am Fuß des Blankeneser Treppenviertels. Der Weg ins Treppenlabyrinth ist bestückt mit Parks und architektonischen Perlen entlang dem Geesthügel. Dichter aber als auf dem Blankeneser Bulln, einem Schwimmponton

on the opposite side, you would feel transported back to village life in another epoch.

Virtually in the middle of Övelgönne village is where you first come across the lively beach life that is as much a part of Elbe folklore as the Rathaus is of the Alster. One particularly vibrant venue, and a Hamburg icon of casual beach ambience, is the *Strandperle* bar and restaurant. Though actually just a shack by a wooden terrace with a graffiti-covered brick wall at the back, this upscale kiosk attracts fans of relaxed outdoor enjoyment at any time of year. From their vantage point by the water they follow with interest the lively activity in the container port on the opposite side, on the Elbe itself, and along its sandy bank. Meanwhile, fifty metres up the hill the Elbchaussee narrows into a bottleneck because creatively parked convertibles and estate cars have given “roadside” a whole new meaning.

Elbe flair for the initiated, with somewhat less hip and hype, is to be found a few kilometres downriver at the foot of the Blankenese Treppenviertel (Staircase Quarter). The way into this labyrinth of staircases is populated with parks and architectural gems on the geest hillside. However, nowhere can you be closer to the

Okay, die Elbe ist auf der anderen Seite. Doch der Uferweg von Övelgönne besitzt so viel Charme, dass man den Blick kaum wenden mag von den alten Kapitäns- und Lotsenhäusern mit ihren schiffigen Exponaten, die einst der Großvater von seinen Reisen nach den Niederländischen Antillen mitbrachte. Oder so ähnlich …

OK, here the Elbe is to the left. Yet the riverside path from Övelgönne has so much charm that you can hardly take your eyes off the old captains' and pilots' houses with maritime exhibits that granddad brought back from his travels to the Dutch Antilles, or some such far-off place.

Wochenend und Sonnenschein ... Reges Strandleben herrscht am Övelgönner Elbufer. Und reger Schiffsverkehr davor, mit Farbexplosion in Rot. Links im Bild das ehemalige Feuerschiff *Elbe 3* von 1888.

Weekend and sunshine ... lively beach life is what it's about on the Övelgönne bank of the Elbe. And in front of it lively shipping traffic, with an explosion of colour in red. To the left in the picture is the former lightship *Elbe 3,* built in 1888.

Von links oben im Uhrzeigersinn: Achtung, Wellengang – Strandburgenbau ist erlaubt am Elbufer, Baden jedoch mit Vorsicht zu genießen. Der Geesthang bei Övelgönne mit der legendären *Strandperle* (rechts unten). Weiter elbabwärts wartet der „Alte Schwede", ein Urgestein aus der letzten Eiszeit, stoisch auf Klettermaxe.

Clockwise from top left: Watch out for the waves – sandcastle building is allowed on the bank of the Elbe, but bathing is to be enjoyed with caution. The geest slope at Övelgönne with the legendary *Strandperle* (below right). Further downstream is the "Alter Schwede," a boulder imported during the last Ice Age which stoically withstands being clambered over.

aus Beton, kann man ohne Boot nicht dran sein an der Elbe. Ein Ort mit rauem Charme, an dem die Seele fliegen darf – ganz ohne künstliche Wellness aus dem Hotelkatalog.
Was kann schöner sein, als auf diesem Schiffsanleger zu sitzen, ein Glas Rot- oder Glühwein vor sich, je nach Jahreszeit, und bei chilliger Musik dem Sonnenuntergang hinterherzuschauen? Oder der Fähre *Altona*, die Besucher über die Elbe schippert, nach Cranz und zu den Obstplantagen ins Alte Land? Containerriesen, Kreuzfahrtschiffe und die kraftstrotzenden Schlepper fahren mitten durchs Bild und bringen mit ihren Bug- und Heckwellen den Ponton zum Schaukeln, ein Gefühl, als sei man selbst mit an Bord. Dazwischen gemütliche karweelbeplankte Tuckerboote und frech und wendig die Freizeitsegler, die unter Aufsicht des rot-weiß geringelten Leuchtturms mit den Riesenpötten um Wind und Wellen konkurrieren.
Als wäre all das nicht genug des Glücks, klettert quasi hinterrücks das Blankeneser Treppenviertel den Elbhang hinauf, eine fast mediterrane Erscheinung. Seepockengleich klammern sich weiße Häuser und Häuschen an das steile Gestade, durchzogen von schmalen

river without a boat than on the Blankenese Bulln, a concrete pontoon bridge. This is a place of raw charm where the soul can be uplifted without any artificial wellness treatments out of a hotel catalogue.
What can be better than to sit on this jetty with a glass of red or mulled wine in front of you, depending on the season, and watch the sunset to a backdrop of relaxing music? Or to watch the *Altona* ferry that sails visitors across the Elbe to Cranz and the orchards in the Altes Land area? Giant container carriers, cruise ships and tugs bursting with energy travel across the middle of the picture. The wash from bow and stern shakes the jetty and makes you feel as if you were on board yourself. Amidst all this are cosy carvel-planked tucker boats and daring, nimble amateur sailors who, under the supervision of the red and white-ringed lighthouse, compete with gigantic ships for wind and waves.
As if that were not happiness enough, the Blankenese Staircase Quarter climbs the slope overlooking the Elbe backwards, as it were, looking almost Mediterranean. White houses and cottages cling like barnacles to the steep bank crisscrossed by a confusion of narrow roads, alleys, staircases and steps around which only

In der zweiten Reihe ist das hohe Elbufer ein Traum in Grün und Weiß. Von links oben im Uhrzeigersinn: der Internationale Seegerichtshof an der Elbchaussee, das Jenisch Haus im gleichnamigen Park, der Katharinenhof in Baurs Park und das Godeffroy-Haus, ein Christian-Frederik-Hansen-Bau von 1789 im Blankeneser Hirschpark.

In the second row, the high bank of the Elbe is a dream in green and white. Clockwise from top left: the International Tribunal for the Law of the Sea on Elbchaussee, the Jenisch Haus in Jenisch Park, the Katharinenhof in Baurs Park and the 1789 Godeffroy-Haus built by Christian Frederik Hansen in the Hirschpark in Blankenese.

Dem Himmel ganz nah: der villengeschmückte grüngesprenkelte Hügel des Blankeneser Treppenviertels über der Elbinsel Schweinesand mit Neßsand. Ganz oben lugen auf 74,4 Metern über Normalnull Turm und Türmchen des eleganten *Süllberg Hotels* hervor, von dessen mehrstufiger Terrasse mit Biergarten man einen der schönsten Blicke über den Strom genießt.

Close to heaven: the villa-adorned, green-sprinkled hill of Blankenese's Staircase Quarter above the Elbe island of Schweinesand with Nesssand. Right at the top, at 74.4 metres above sea level, the tower and turret of the elegant *Süllberg Hotel* peep out. From its stepped terrace and beer garden you can enjoy one of the finest views of the river.

Rosenumrankt und unter Reet hat das historische Fischerhaus seinen Platz an der Sonne auf dem Blankeneser Hügel. Heute Heimatmuseum und Treffpunkt, diente das „Dreehus“ in früheren Zeiten drei Familien als Wohnstatt, Fachwerk und „Klöntür“ für den windgeschützten „Schnack“ inklusive.

With its climbing roses and thatched roof, this historic fishermen’s cottage has its place in the sun on the Blankenese hill. Now a local history museum and meeting place, in former times the “Dreehus” was home to three families. It features half-timbering and a “Klöntür,” stable-type door to provide shelter from the wind while people stood and chatted.

Oben links, unten rechts: Diese Kiosk-Kneipen sind Kult im „Dorf“, wie die Blankeneser ihren Stadtteil nennen. In der *Kajüte S.B.12* sitzt man mit den Füßen im Sand, vorm *Ponton op’n Bulln* baumeln sie fast in der Elbe. Dazu der schönste Bauerngarten am Strandweg und das Treppenviertel vom Wasser aus gesehen.

Top left, bottom right: These kiosk pubs are all the go in the village, as Blankeneser locals call their district. At the *Kajüte S.B.12* you sit with your feet in the sand, while in front of the *Ponton op’n Bulln* they almost dangle in the Elbe. Also pictured are the most beautiful cottage garden on Strandweg, and a view of the Staircase Quarter from the water.

Gassen, Gängen, Treppen und Stiegen, in deren Gewirr sich nur die Alteingesessenen wirklich auskennen. Winzig die Gärten, dafür mit Aussicht. Feigenbäume wachsen über Mauern, Stockrosen zwischen den Pflasterritzen. Griechenland? Dänemark? Nein: Bullerbü auf Hanseatisch. Und fürs „Alpen light"-Gefühl sorgt der hotelgekrönte Süllberg mit Aussicht über die Elbinseln bis nach Niedersachsen und Schleswig-Holstein.
Spätestens an dieser Stelle sind wir wieder beim Himmel auf Erden.

longstanding residents really know their way. Gardens are tiny, but have views. Fig trees grow over walls, hollyhocks in cracks in the pavement. Greece? Denmark? No. This is Astrid Lindgren's famous children's book idyll 'Bullerby' – but in the Hanseatic style. Meanwhile, the "Alps light" effect is provided by the hotel-topped Süllberg with its view across the Elbe islands to Lower Saxony and Schleswig-Holstein.
Here, if not before, we are back in heaven on earth.

Blankeneser Abendstimmung mit Insel und Leuchtturm. Muss man da wirklich noch woandershin? Nö.

Evening mood in Blankenese with island and lighthouse. Is there really any need to go anywhere else? No, or Nö, as they say in Hamburg.

Autorin, Bildnachweis, Impressum/
Author, Photo credits, Imprint

Autorin/Author
Karin Baron, geb. 1958, studierte Angewandte Sprach- und Kulturwissenschaften in Germersheim, Genf und London. Sie arbeitete als Übersetzerin, Redakteurin und Texterin und ist Autorin zahlreicher Kinder- und Jugendbücher. Ihr halbes Leben lang wohnt sie in Hamburg, möchte dort nicht mehr weg und muss einmal pro Woche Elbsand unter den Füßen haben. Im Ellert & Richter Verlag erschien ihr Buch *Wo Hamburg am schönsten ist* (2016).

Karin Baron, born in 1958, studied Applied Linguistics and Cultural Studies in Germersheim, Geneva and London. She worked as a translator, editor and copywriter and is the author of numerous books for children and young people. She has lived half her life in Hamburg, never wants to leave it, and needs to feel Elbe sand beneath her feet once a week. Her book *Wo Hamburg am schönsten* ist was published by Ellert & Richter Verlag in 2016.

Bildnachweis/Photo credits
Fotolia: 6 o.l., 8/9, 30/31, 36, 37, 41, 43, 45 o.r., 48/49, 67. Ottmar Heinze, Hamburg: 59 u.l. Huber-images: 6 u.r., 12 r., 14, 15 o.l., 33, 71 u.r., 73 o.r., 76, 77 o.l.+o.r.+u.l. (Bäck); 6 u.l., 47 u.l., 53 o.l.+o.r. (Croppi Gabriele); 27 u.r. (Forster Stuart); Titel, 17, 18, 20, 22, 24/25, 28, 34, 55, 69, 71 o.r. (Gräfenhain); 23 u.l., 27 o.r., 27 u.l., 61 (Merten Hans-Peter); 10, 23 o.r., 35 r. (Rellini Maurizio); 23 u.r., 47 r. (TC). Urs Kluyver, Hamburg: 5, 6 o.r., 7, 12 o.l. +u.l., 13, 15 o.r.+u.l.+u.r., 19, 23 o.l., 27 o.l., 29, 35 o.l.+u.l., 38, 45 l.+ u.r., 46, 50 o.l.+o.r.+u.r., 52, 53 u.l., 59 o.l., 64/65, 70, 71 o.l.+u.l., 73 o.l.+ u.l., 74/75, 77 u.r. Egbert Kossak, Hamburg: 47 o.l., 62, 63. Katrin Schmersahl, Hamburg: 73 u.r., 79. Wikimedia Commons (CC-BY-SA): 40 o.l. (3.0 Sergej Medvedev), 40 u.l. (3.0de Ajepah), 40 r. (3.0 Ajepah), 50 u.l. (2.0 Florian Timm), 56 (3.0de NordNordWest), 59 r. (3.0 San Andreas)

Titelbild/Cover: Elbphilharmonie, Hamburg (huber-images/Gräfenhain)

Bibliografische Information der Deutschen Nationalbibliothek
Die Deutsche Nationalbibliothek verzeichnet diese Publikation in der Deutschen Nationalbibliografie; detaillierte bibliografische Daten sind im Internet über http://dnb.d-nb.de abrufbar.

ISBN 978-3-8319-0678-9

3. Auflage 2019

Text und Bildunterschriften/Text and captions: Karin Baron, Hamburg
Lektorat/Editor: Annette Krüger, Hamburg
Übersetzung ins Englische/English translation: Mary Tyler, London
Gestaltung/Design: BrücknerAping Büro für Gestaltung GbR, Bremen
Gesamtherstellung/Production: Printvit, Breslau

www.ellert-richter.de
www.facebook.com/EllertRichterVerlag